D0856840

	DATE DUE		

J. S. MILL IN 90 MINUTES

J. S. Mill
IN 90 MINUTES

Paul Strathern

IVAN R. DEE
CHICAGO

Library of Congress Cataloging-in-Publication Data:
Strathern, Paul, 1940–
      J.S. Mill in 90 minutes / Paul Strathern.
          p. cm. — (Philosophers in 90 minutes)
      Includes bibliographical references and index.
      ISBN 1-56663-474-1 (cloth : alk. paper) —
  ISBN 1-56663-473-3 (paper : alk. paper)
      1. Mill, John Stuart, 1806–1873. I. Title: J.S. Mill in
  ninety minutes. II. Title. III. Series.

  B1607 .S79 2002
  192—dc21
  [B]   2002073674

Contents

J. S. MILL IN 90 MINUTES

Introduction

"The greatest happiness of the greatest number is the foundation of morals and legislation."
　　　　—The "Sacred Truth" of Utilitarianism

John Stuart Mill is best remembered today as the leading exponent of Utilitarianism, but he did not invent this philosophy or even initiate its wide-ranging influence. This was the work of the remarkable Jeremy Bentham.

In his later years John Stuart Mill wrote a perceptive portrait of Bentham: "He had neither internal experience, nor external. He never knew prosperity and adversity, passion nor satiety; he never had even the experience which sickness gives; he lived from childhood to the age of eighty-five in boyish health. He knew no dejection, no heaviness of heart. He never felt life a sore and weary burthen. He was a boy to the last."

Bentham's family bequeathed him sufficient cash to live on for the rest of his life without working. He put this stroke of fortune to exceptional use. He devoted his entire life to thought. Yet not all this thinking involved philosophy and theoretical matters. The progressive Utilitarian ideal that he founded permeated all his thinking. Bentham sought progress in all fields, from politics to prisons, from philosophy to frozen peas. His most celebrated practical scheme was the Panopticon, a revolutionary new design for a prison. This was laid out like a wheel, with the cells lining the outer rim and the warder's tower at the axle. This panoptic (all-seeing) tower enabled the warden to look into all the cells without going on patrol. Yet the architecture of this efficient prison was not the only novel feature. Bentham proposed that his prison should be run as a profit-making business. In this way it could be self-supporting, and the hard work involved for the prisoners would "grind the rogues honest." But this process would also prove humane—for the governor would feed the prisoners well and keep them in good health, so that they could work harder and earn more money. Bentham became so enamored of this scheme, and ran up such debts while attempting to persuade the government to adopt it, that he almost ended up in jail himself—as a bankrupt. His acquaintance with the bankruptcy laws (which could still inflict forty-eight hours pillory in the stocks and the cutting off of ears) proved a sobering shock.

Bentham's other practical schemes ranged from an early form of telephone (involving a network of speaking tubes) to a project for digging a canal across the Panama isthmus to the Pacific, as well as his celebrated scheme for the freezing of vegetables so that peas could be served for Christmas dinner. Other projects included law reform, emancipation of the colonies, the drawing up of a British constitution, the establishment of London University, and, last but not least, a wholescale and radical overhaul of the bankruptcy laws.

Bentham spent much of his life badgering the authorities. But not in person. He was a shy man who preferred to live a secluded life devoted to his schemes and ideas, attended only by his loyal friends and disciples. Among these was James Mill, John Stuart Mill's father. This group, known as the "philosophical radicals," promoted Bentham's work in public. Their advocacy of his ideas had widespread effect, especially in Parliament, where Bentham's allies included David Ricardo, the great classical economist of his day. Even Bentham's constant stream of pestering letters to the authorities would (sometimes inadvertently) bring about major reforms. In the course of his correspondence with the governor of the Bank of England about an unforgeable banknote that he had recently dreamed up, Bentham happened to inquire precisely how many banknotes were in circulation. The governor realized that he had no idea. Nor did anyone else in the Bank. If it was to persist in any plausible claim to be in control of the currency, the Bank realized that it had better start by finding out how much of this unknown entity there was. In this way Jeremy Bentham can claim responsibility for the introduction of the numbering on English banknotes—as well as the first monetary policy that actually had some idea of what it was talking about.

Yet Bentham was far from merely a brilliant crackpot. All his multifarious schemes and projects were guided by a central principle—his Utilitarian idea. This was built upon the following idea: "Nature has placed mankind under the governance of two sovereign masters, *pain* and *pleasure*. It is in them alone to point out what we ought to do, as well as what we shall do." Such an enlightened and humane idea was regarded as radical at the time. The fact that it now appears obvious to us is largely the result of Bentham, James Mill, and his son John Stuart Mill, as well as their Utilitarian colleagues. What we tend to accept as self-evident was far from being so in most societies throughout history and remains so in more than a few today. The implications of Bentham's Utilitarian ideal would lead directly to the belief in democratic liberalism that permeates free Western society.

Bentham's Utilitarianism was based upon what he called the "sacred truth." This proclaimed: "The greatest happiness of the greatest number is the foundation of morals and legislation." His aim was to make his philosophy, and with it the principles of the social sciences, as rigid as the laws of natural science. He saw Utilitarianism and its pleasure principle as the new gravity of morality, as a result he confidently expected that one day he would be recognized as the Newton of the social sciences and philosophy. His basic argument was based upon the "principle of utility" that he saw as a moral principle. What gives us pleasure is good, what gives us pain is evil. But for such a principle to be moral it must be viewed in social terms. What is right maximizes everyone's pleasure, what is wrong causes an overall increase in pain and suffering. When confronted with difficult decisions, we must weigh up the net pleasure against the net pain.

This brings us to the main difficulty of Utilitarianism. How is it possible to measure pleasure, either on the individual or the collective scale? Bentham tackled this problem in some detail, coming up with his "felicific calculus" for the precise measurement of pleasure. In his analysis he listed seven different dimensions of pleasure, including its duration and the number of individuals affected by it. He also listed fourteen different types of simple pleasures, ranging through those resulting from power, wealth, skill, good name, and, last but not least, malevolence. Likewise he named a dozen "simple pains," ranging from disappointment to desire (a category that would seem to render most of us masochists). But the plain fact is that pleasure, whether solitary or social, remains beyond precise quantification. And this remains so, even now that we can investigate it at the biological level. There is no fixed scale by which intensity of stimulus can be universally related to consequent enjoyment. An Indian fakir may enjoy a curry, or a bed of nails, which a Dane finds intolerable.

Bentham worked closely with James Mill and took a keen interest in his son John Stuart. Soon both would come to see John Stuart Mill as Bentham's natural heir, the ideal choice to carry forward the torch of Bentham's ideas into the next generation.

Bentham died on June 6th, 1832, just two days after the passing of the Reform Bill which he had done so much to encourage. This bill would transform the political face of Britain, extending the franchise to take account of the new urban centers that had mushroomed with the Industrial Revolution. This was not yet democracy as we know it; much of the lower middle class and all the working class still remained without a vote. Yet it is now seen as the beginning of the inexorable move toward universal democracy in Britain, which would be achieved within a century.

Bentham's death was every bit as extraordinary as his life. His "modern scientific" will specified that at his funeral his body should be dissected in the presence of his mourning friends. His filleted remains were then to be embalmed, dressed in his favorite walking clothes and straw hat, and exhibited in a glass case. This "auto-icon," as he called it, would be far more exact and fitting a memorial than any statue. True to his wishes, this ghoulish sight can now be seen preserved in a glass case at University College, London, which he did so much to found. (Students, acting upon their own version of Bentham's pleasure principle, manage to "liberate" his mummified head every few years.)

Mill's Life and Works

John Stuart Mill was born in London on May 20, 1806. From his earliest years his education was carried out by his father: James Mill was determined to turn his son into a genius. At the age of three, young John Stuart began studying arithmetic and ancient Greek. By eight he was launched into Latin, algebra, and geometry; by twelve he was deemed ready for logic and philosophy. But not everything went according to plan. Apparently at the age of seven young Mill read Plato's *Theaetetus* in the original Greek. Although he understood the words and could follow the sentences, he found that he somehow failed to grasp the gist of the work. Considering that this high-minded dialogue of Plato's is devoted to a lengthy discussion of the finer points of how knowledge itself should be defined, the child's puzzlement is not surprising. Not so to James Mill, who instructed him to read it again.

Regardless and relentless, the child's indoctrination began at six o'clock each morning, continuing throughout the day. He was isolated from all frivolous contact with other children and was allowed no holidays "lest the habit of work should be broken and a taste for idleness acquired." Poetry was forbidden and imagination discouraged. Mill senior believed that private emotion should be suppressed in favor of restrained public expressions of general social approbation or displeasure. His guiding spirit was Walter Landor's maxim: "Few acquaintances, fewer friends, no familiarities." James Mill—the leading public champion of Bentham's pleasure principle and the benign mentor of the great economic thinker Ricardo—was in fact a classic Victorian monster in the privacy of his own home. His obsession with his son's education knew no bounds. By the age of thirteen

John Stuart Mill had in his own words finished "a complete course in political economy." This was no exaggeration: he would now sit in on discussions between his father and Ricardo, absorbing the very latest economic ideas, even occasionally making his own astute contributions.

In 1821 the fifteen-year-old Mill came across Bentham's *Treatise on Morals and Legislation.* By the time he had finished reading through this three-volume work, "I had become a different human being." His admiration for Bentham and his Utilitarian ideas knew no bounds. "From now on I had what might truly be called an object in life; to be a reformer of the world."

Bentham was never much interested in publication. He left it to his disciples to put together finished books out of his daily production of unfinished treatises and passing thoughts on every subject that took his fancy. At the age of eighteen John Stuart Mill embarked upon the mammoth task of piecing together thousands of scraps of paper, covered with Bentham's scrawled handwriting, into a consecutive manuscript of more than a million words. This would eventually emerge as the multivolume work *On Evidence.*

As Mill later tellingly remarked in his *Autobiography,* "I was never a boy." One can imagine the domestic atmosphere presided over by a man described by his son: "for passionate emotion of all sorts . . . he professed the greatest contempt. He regarded them as a form of madness." But what did young Mill's mother make of all this? Either through fear, weakness, or resignation, she did nothing. She had evidently seen it all before: her mother had run an asylum. Indicatively, John Stuart Mill does not mention his mother once during the entire 325 pages of his *Autobiography.*

So successful was James Mill's brainwashing of his son that by the age of twenty even John Stuart's inner life was governed utterly by reason. He could allow himself no deviation from the tyranny of his indoctrinated mind. He even seems to have remained unaware of his exceptional talents, judging them to be "below rather than above par, what I could do could assuredly be done by any boy or girl of average capacity."

Such a judgment could only have come from someone who had simply never met—or freely conversed—with someone of his own age. Even so, a growing self-awareness gradually began to dawn in the young man who had never been a boy. Working obsessively as ever amidst the gloom of a foggy London autumn day in 1826, he found himself pausing to ask himself: "Suppose that all your objects in life were realized . . . would this be a great joy and happiness to you?" In his own words: "An irrepressible self-consciousness distinctly answered, 'No!' At this my heart sank within me: the whole foundation on which my life was constructed fell down." The young man who believed utterly in the philosophy of happiness was incapable of achieving this for himself.

John Stuart Mill was having a long-overdue nervous breakdown. Typically he appears to have kept this to himself. Even more typically, neither his mother nor his father seems to have noticed. Yet amidst the inner turmoil a sea change was taking place. Mill began reading the romantic poetry of Wordsworth and the writings of irra-

tional thinkers such as the French social reformer Saint-Simon. Then one day he found
himself "accidentally" reading the *Mémoires* of
the sentimental French poet Jean-François Mar-
montel. When he came to the passage where the
poet describes the death of his father, Mill burst
into tears. He claimed that he was moved by his
own "vivid conception" of the scene, though he
makes no reference to what was actually taking
place in it. His suppressed wish that such a scene
should take place in his own life would not have
been so transparent in those pre-Freudian times.
Mill concluded that he was now cured: "The op-
pression of the thought that all feeling was dead
within me, was gone." John Stuart Mill would
now devote himself to the introduction of
humanity into his philosophy.

Although he retained his belief in the Utilitarian principle, Mill began to form critical judg-
ments of its founders. Regarding Bentham, he
realized: "Self-consciousness, that demon of the
men of genius of our time [that is, the Romantics
such as Wordsworth] never was awakened in
him." He concluded that Bentham belonged to

22

"a generation of the leanest and barrenest men whom England had ever produced." This latter comment betrays more than a hint of subconscious antagonism toward his father. Yet at the same time he still believed that Bentham was "a great benefactor of mankind." Besides introducing a human element, Mill would also seek to broaden the whole concept of Utilitarianism. In doing so he would transform what had begun as a far-reaching and ameliorative liberal idea into a distinct and logically argued philosophy.

Despite his pronouncement that he was cured, Mill only gradually recovered from his breakdown. He now courted his father's disapproval by attending classical concerts. Yet in the midst of an enjoyable performance his overheated logical mind would be gripped with the fear that all music must inevitably come to an end. It had only a limited number of notes, and these would surely soon all be used up. (Despite this simple blunder, Mill's exceptional logical powers were fortunately restored along with his sanity.)

The inevitably somewhat priggish, driven,

and extraordinarily precocious young man whom Mill had been, emerged from his mental ordeal as a human being of rare quality. In place of the unimaginative rigidity instilled by his father, he became an exceptionally understanding man, habitually able to see and empathize with the other person's point of view. His nobility of purpose was now tempered by practicality. He developed a wide feeling for what human happiness means and a contempt for narrow and unforgiving sectarianism.

Then the inevitable happened. At the age of twenty-four he fell in love with a woman he found darkly attractive and highly intelligent. The twenty-two-year-old Harriet Taylor was a poet of turbulent but contained emotion, and she immediately reciprocated his love. Unfortunately she was also married—to an energetic and successful businessman, whose exceptional qualities of understanding turned out to be the match of Mill's. John Taylor loved his wife but was quickly persuaded by his forceful partner that she loved John Stuart Mill. Harriet's sense of loyalty to her husband—for whom she retained a deep fondness—made her assure him that while she insisted upon seeing her lover, there would be no "impropriety" between them. Within a year Queen Victoria had ascended the British throne: meanwhile this very Victorian state of affairs would continue for another *twenty years*.

Mill took to seeing Harriet Taylor regularly, sometimes even staying for the weekend when John Taylor was away on business. When such occasions did not arise, John Taylor would tactfully retire to his club after dinner, and his wife's lover would turn up for a platonic evening of earnest philosophic discussion and poetry. Over the years John Taylor developed a certain irritability, John Stuart Mill developed a pronounced tic in one eyebrow, and Harriet herself was beset by a series of nervous complaints—but otherwise all remained swimmingly smooth on the surface. Exercising their powers of sublimation to the utmost, the well-tried trio succeeded in their chosen paths. Taylor made money in the chemical business, Mill became an exceptional philosopher, and Harriet played a major role in developing his ideas. (Mill later claimed that she co-wrote many of his major works.) Meanwhile the Victorian gossips had a field day. Mill would cut dead any friend who even so much as mentioned the name of his lover; Taylor took to enjoying bibulous institutional dinners; and Harriet developed a remarkable ability to faint.

Mill continued with his habit of strenuous work. At eighteen he had entered the civil service, taking a post at the East India Company where his father was a senior official. (James Mill was not about to allow his son to squander his intellectual heritage at a university.) A few years later John Stuart Mill also took on the task of editing the influential *Westminster Review*, which attracted such writers as Coleridge and George Eliot. (Among this magazine's many philosophical and literary achievements were the introduction of Kant to general English readership and a review of the unknown Schopenhauer, which overnight made him belatedly famous in Germany.)

By now Bentham's presence had been reduced to a ghoulish mummified figure in a glass case, and in 1836 James Mill lay dying. Where-upon John Stuart Mill suffered another nervous breakdown. Indicatively, this rendered him unable to visit his father during his last days. After the death of James Mill, his son once again recovered—the twitch in his eyebrow now more pronounced than ever.

In 1843 John Stuart Mill published *System of Logic,* the work which established his name. It follows in the British empiricist tradition of Locke, Berkeley, and Hume but disregards the subsequent German metaphysical philosophies developed by Kant and Hegel. (Metaphysics Mill was content to dismiss, but *German* metaphysics was one of the few subjects that provoked him to passionate outbursts. He even declared that being conversant with Hegel "tends to deprave one's intellect.") Mill's empiricism laid the philosophical ground on which he would base the Utilitarian idea. In line with the empiricists, Mill maintained that we derive all our knowledge ultimately from experience. This derivation may involve the use of reason, but even reasoning itself is also derived from experience. In the historical, psychological, and philosophical senses, we discover reason by means of enumerative induction. That is, we make generalizations, which are *induced* by repetitive *enumeration*. We observe occurrence A (the sun) appearing to cause occurrence B (melting ice). We then observe this time and again. So we conclude that A causes B (sun melts ice.) According to Mill, this is the way all scientific thinking works: it generates laws out of experimental experience.

Mill well recognized that induction is fallible. No matter how many times we witness a similar sequence of events, we can never know for certain that next time something different will not occur. The statement "All swans are white" had always been accepted as true; but with the discovery and European settlement of Australia in the late eighteenth and early nineteenth centuries, it came to light that black swans too existed. The possibility of error always persisted in inductively generated knowledge. Nevertheless Mill insisted that such knowledge could have different degrees of reliability. This too could be demonstrated empirically, from how we acquired such knowledge and what kind of evidence it produced. If the knowledge proved useful in generating further knowledge, it showed that it had a higher degree of certainty. General patterns of experience could give rise to "laws" of nature, which in turn could prove fruitful in determining further laws of nature. The fact that many acids reacted with alkalis to produce salts led chemists to the hypothesis that perhaps all acids were potentially capable of reaction with alkalis to produce salts. This could then be tested, and many more particular reactions could be discovered in the process.

Such evaluation of certainty could occur even in unscientific fields. Initially our induction about a particular sequence of events is spontaneous. For instance, we discover that drinking a large amount of beer makes us drunk. Later this sequence is repeated again and again, and it forms a coherent pattern with our other experience. Drinking a large amount of cider or wine or whiskey also makes us drunk. This leads us to second-order inductions: drinking large amounts of any alcohol makes us drunk.

More important, we also generate second-order inductive conclusions concerning *all* our experience. In the light of our repetetive experiences, we induce that all phenomena are subject to an overall conformity. Their behavior will be consistent with previous behavior. We conclude that nature itself conforms to certain overall laws. As a result of repeated and widespread experience, we conclude that every effect has a cause. This conclusion is reached historically at a certain point in our lives; it becomes part of our psychological apparatus, and it goes on to inform our entire philosophical outlook. It becomes the way we live, the way we are, and the way we think.

Having reached this conclusion about causation, we can then take a step forward into further scientific discovery through "eliminative induction." We experience an event and discover several possible causes for it. Someone dies: we examine all possible causes. A species becomes extinct: we search for, and disregard, particular causes. One by one the different causes are eliminated until we arrive at the induced ("correct")

30

answer. In turn this has the reflective effect of re-inforcing our individual belief in the law of causation. But as we can see, even this eliminative induction is firmly based upon the prior principle of enumerative induction.

In Mill's view, enumerative induction ultimately accounts for the whole of our scientific knowledge. In the end we rely upon this method, which makes use of just two basic elements—experience and memory.

Mill's argument has great force but retains certain weaknesses. Despite second-order inductions—such as consistency and causation—his argument does not overcome the radical empiricism of Hume with regard to the future. All our inductive knowledge relies upon more than simple past and present consistency. It also relies upon our assumption that the *future* will be consistent with the past and the present. For Mill, the assumption that the future will resemble the past belongs to our second-order inductive knowledge. But this contains a logical circularity. It is not possible for any induction to indicate that the the future will be the same as the past or the present—for the simple reason that the entire inductive process is founded upon this assumption!

A second objection comes from scientists themselves. The method they use to discover new laws really has little or nothing to do with induction. A scientist examines the perplexing facts and then puts forward a *hypothesis* to explain them. This he then tests, to see if it fits the facts. If it does, the hypothesis is accepted as knowledge, a scientific law, or even a law of nature. Yet Mill's counter to this charge also contains a certain force. In his view, any hypothesis will always remain highly uncertain. There may well be other hypotheses that also fit all the facts. The hypothetical method provides no guidance about which hypothesis to accept. (Despite Mill's cavil, any overlapping second-order inductions from enumerative induction suffer from just the same defect.)

Mill's empirical method also leaves him open to another damaging question: How do we know that the phenomena we experience exist independently of our experience of them? In other words, how do know there is such a thing as a real and persisting world? Mill consistently refused to hypothesize that a permanent world exists beyond our consciousness of it. Instead he suggested that "matter" may be regarded as "a permanent possibility of sensation." He felt confident "that this conception of matter includes the whole meaning attached to it by the common world." Other co-inhabitants of this common world may find themselves less convinced. In complementary fashion Mill went on to argue that the mind is a "permanent possibility of having sensation." Our mind is a series of feelings and sensations which can become aware of itself as a "thread of consciousness." Working its way backward along this thread provides the mind with memories.

This argument is not a particularly convincing explanation of what happens, either psychologically or philosophically. Yet the phrase "thread of consciousness" was in its own way highly prescient. It would be another half-century before the American psychologist William James produced the more satisfactory description of the mind and its "stream of consciousness." Mill may have provided the first step toward this imaginative and illuminating conception.

According to Mill, we discover the laws of logic by enumerative induction. Such laws as the law of identity—a thing cannot be itself and something else at the same time—arise as second-order inductions from everyday experience. Similarly, the laws of mathematics derive from our inductive knowledge of phenomena. The number one is a generalization derived from observation of single objects. Likewise, the number two is a generalization derived from our observation of pairs of objects. These two separate generalizations are not essentially linked, or built up from a series of basic mathematical axioms. This means that 1 + 1 = 2 is simply an induction from experience. It is in no way logically or arithmetically "necessary." It is induced knowledge, on a par with "All swans are white." Indeed, according to Mill's view it is quite possible that on some future occasion we will discover that 1 + 1 does not equal 2. But because we have a vast quantity of experience confirming our induction that 1 + 1 = 2, we are highly certain of its truth.

Here Mill was in fact arguing against the view that had been held by his father, who had been a nominalist with regard to mathematics. According to James Mill, 1 + 1 is simply a *definition* of 2. The whole of mathematics was built upon the basis of such simple definitions. John Stuart Mill also faced the wrath of many nineteenth-century mathematicians, including the formidable Cambridge professor William Whewell, who took the intuitionist view. According to the intuitionists, we simply cannot conceive of how 1 + 1 could not equal 2. It is literally unthinkable. Thus 1 + 1 *does* equal two: it must, there is no other way. The whole of mathematics was built upon the utter certainty of such basic intuitions.

Mill countered this by pointing out that our knowledge of the world was now filled with notions that had previously been considered inconceivable. Throughout the Middle Ages it had been inconceivable that the earth was spherical and orbited the sun. Until Newton's observation of gravity, it had been inconceivable that the earth acted over a vast distance to influence the movement of the moon.

But Mill's empirical view of mathematics encounters several difficulties. The main problem with relating numbers to empirical knowledge is the very nature of mathematics. In the universe of our experience is a finite number of objects; on the other hand, we know that there are infinitely many arithmetical numbers. A similar objection arose from the new geometry, which had recently been discovered by the Russian mathematician Lobachevsky and would prove a crippling blow to the empiricist view of mathematics. Lobachevsky had shown that Euclidian geometry, which applied to plane (or flat) surfaces, was not the only form of geometry. There were other entirely different geometries which applied to curved surfaces. These often had no correlate in the physical world. Mathematical space and physical space were in no way identical: here experience and mathematics were two entirely different things.

In 1844 Mill turned his attention to economics, or political economy as it was then known. The subject was still in its infancy. Adam Smith had published the founding work of the discipline, *The Wealth of Nations,* just seventy years earlier.

In the *Principles of Political Economy,* Mill generally follows the economic principles first set down by Smith and later developed by Ricardo. This tradition came to be known as "classical economics." But Mill also made several important discoveries which would change this classical tradition forever. The most profound of these was the most simple: Mill realized that the laws that govern economics are concerned with production, not with distribution. The productivity of labor, of the soil, of machinery—these can all be organized more or less efficiently according to certain objective laws. These laws are affected by certain limiting factors, such as nature (glut or famine), productivity (of labor, of machine), and so forth. Wealth is thus produced according to laws and objective factors which enable us to maximize its quantity. But once it has been produced, there is no way we can "maximize" its distribution.

Before this, Smith, Ricardo, and their follow-ers had simply absolved themselves when con-fronted with the consequences of the economic laws they discovered. The free market had its own "natural" laws, and nothing could be done about them. In a glut, prices dropped—and wages were bound to follow suit. As arable land became more scarce, rent went up. It was as sim-ple as that, no matter the suffering involved. Mill's uncoupling of production and distribution brought an end to such natural laws where dis-tribution was concerned. Once wealth had been produced, once goods were ready for market, "mankind, individually or collectively, can do with them as they please. They can place them at the disposal of whomsoever they please and on whatever terms." Distribution had no "natural" laws. "The rules by which it is determined are what the opinions and feelings of the ruling por-tion of the community make them, and are very different in different ages and countries, and might be still more different if mankind so

38

chose." With distribution, morality became a factor. Mill had shown how ethics could find its way into capitalist economics.

This was an original insight. It was very different from the nineteenth-century socialists and Mill's contemporary, Marx (who published his *Communist Manifesto* in the very same year that Mill published his *Principles of Political Economy*). Marx and the socialists sought to introduce morality into economics by changing the entire free-market economic system into a controlled socialist system. Mill, on the other hand, introduced morality into the very citadel of capitalism. Having first uncoupled production from distribution, he then suggested that Utilitarian principles be applied where the distribution of wealth was concerned.

The distribution of wealth was at that time very much the polar opposite of Utilitarianism. It seemed designed to produce the greatest misery of the greatest number. Mill was no revolutionary, he had no wish to destroy the system. His ideas were intended to transform the system by making it better for all concerned. Utilitarianism was arguably the first ethical philosophy that could be applied to the complexity of modern commerce without appearing naive, simplistic, or inadequate. It would not transform economic society overnight, yet its creeping influence would extend ever further during the ensuing 150 years to the present. Although not acknowledged as such, Utilitarianism remains at least the guiding principle in all labor-market bargaining, union negotiations, and executive salary levels. It may not be adhered to, but it undeniably *informs* all such social interaction—it is the one common denominator. It remains a yardstick by which most of us judge the distribution of wealth. Ludicrously inflated earnings for senior executives of large corporations are said to be "what the market dictates." This is seen as a matter of production, beyond moral debate. Objections to such practice make use of Mill's original distinction and insist that it is a matter of distribution. This means that such remunerations *are* subject to more than simply economic considerations. They fall within the realm of moral judgment. And the most pertinent application here would seem to many to be the Utilitarian idea of the common good.

While Mill was writing his *Principles of Political Economy,* he made a habit of dining with Harriet Taylor at least once a week. He was still deeply in love with her, and would later claim that by this stage she had become so involved with his work as to be his collaborator, producing many original ideas and even writing large sections of his books. In his opinion, Harriet had the mind of a "consummate artist." Indeed, her "sagacity" fitted her to be judged as "eminent amongst the rulers of the mankind." Others, not blinded by love, saw a somewhat different person: an unexceptional, rather vain woman. Whatever the truth, there is no denying that during these years Harriet proved a major inspiration and support for Mill. The precise extent of her contribution is open to question, yet there is no denying that she *did* contribute, and significantly, to the work of one of the most eminent and wide-ranging thinkers of the age. For this reason Harriet Taylor has recently been placed in the pantheon of forerunners of the feminist movement. Mill too would eventually play his part in female emancipation—and, as we shall see, he would undeniably be guided by many of *her* ideas.

In 1849 Harriet's husband died. After a suitable gap of two years, John Stuart Mill finally married Harriet Taylor. They could now share the same home, free from gossip. Yet apart from this, their relationship remained as before. Although it is impossible to know for certain, all the indications are that their marriage was never consummated. Indeed their chaste regard for each other would have had to undergo a traumatic transformation for it to have been otherwise. By this stage, neither was capable of facing up to any hint of physicality in their relationship. Mill's eyebrow went on twitching, and Harriet began suffering from such hypochondria that she became a partial invalid.

In 1858, in the aftermath of the Indian Mutiny, the East India Company was dissolved, and the administration of India was taken over by the government. Mill, as a senior company executive, was able to retire on a sizable pension.

He and Harriet set off for the south of France, hoping that the climate would be good for her health. By now it had become clear that Harriet's "illnesses" were more than psychosomatic. She had tuberculosis (which she may well have caught from Mill himself, who also suffered from the telltale lung-racking cough). When they reached Avignon, Harriet succumbed to a severe fever. Mill could only watch, appalled, as his beloved Harriet rapidly faded away and died.

To alleviate this blow, Mill now buried himself in his work. The most important book he produced during this period was the comparatively short *Utilitarianism*. Published in 1861, it contains the kernel of his philosophy, the central Utilitarianism that informed all his other works.

Mill's early hero-worship of Bentham and the Utilitarian philosophy he had originated were considerably tempered by his early nervous breakdown. It had led Mill to reject many of Bentham's ideas, especially his overemphasis on the rational nature of humanity, and his belief that human behavior was amenable to calculation (the felicific calculus). Such an analytic approach was no way to regard human beings. Firsthand experience had taught Mill that "the habit of analysis tends to wear away the feelings." Bentham had neglected the emotional and spiritual side of society; his Utilitarianism had been limited to enlightened welfarism. This was cold charity. Indeed, Bentham's entire approach to society had been marred by the pseudo-scientific emphasis of the Enlightenment, with its emphasis on reason. He had not taken into account the historical developments and binding passions that had given rise to that society. Mill's Utilitarianism, on the other hand, was influenced by the Romantic writers (such as Wordsworth and Coleridge) as well as by the ancient Greeks. He sought to temper his social attitude with compassion and an understanding of the full range of human behavior. Like the humanity it contained, society was also subject to psychological and emotional forces.

Utilitarianism is essentially based upon a moral principle—that pleasure is good. The strongest argument against morality in philosophy had been put forward in the previous century by Hume. "In every system of morality . . . the author proceeds for some time in the ordinary way of reasoning, and establishes the being of a God, or makes observations concerning human affairs; when of a sudden I am surpriz'd to find, that instead of the usual copulations of propositions, *is*, and *is not*, I meet with no proposition that is not connected with an *ought*, or an *ought not*. The change is imperceptible; but is, however, of the last consequence." Having exposed this underhand reasoning, Hume concludes: "the distinction of vice and virtue is not founded merely on the relations of objects, nor is perceiv'd by reason." Morality is simply a matter of feelings and opinions. It lies beyond the realm of philosophical reasoning. Any philosophy based on morality, such as Utilitarianism, would have to find a way around Hume's argument.

From the outset it is clear that Mill's *Utilitarianism* has a depth and subtlety of argument. "The only proof capable of being given that an object is visible is that people actually see it. The only proof that a sound is audible is that people hear it: and so of the other sources of our experience. In like manner, I apprehend, the sole evidence it is possible to produce that anything is desirable is that people do actually desire it." Then with a skill that is in no way underhand, he proceeds: "desiring a thing and finding it pleasant, aversion to it and thinking of it as painful, are phenomena entirely inseperable, or rather two parts of the same phenomena. . . . To desire anything, except in proportion as the idea of it is pleasant, is a physical and metaphysical impossibility."

Mill is well aware of Hume's argument and seeks to circumvent it. He does not smuggle an *ought* into his argument, where previously there had only been an *is*; instead he presents a *psychological* fact. At this point it is worth reiterating in full Bentham's core Utilitarian principles, to which Mill continued to subscribe: "Nature has placed mankind under the governance of two sovereign masters, *pain* and *pleasure*. It is for them alone to point out what we ought to do, as well as to determine what we shall do. . . . The standard of right and wrong [is] fastened to their throne. They govern us in all we do, in all we say, in all we think: every effort we make to throw off our subjection will serve but to demonstrate and confirm . . . [this] *principle of utility*." Mill concurs: "I regard utility as the ultimate appeal on all ethical questions."

From the outset, Hume's reservation is pertinent to the Utilitarian argument. The principle of utility is undeniably guilty: "Pleasure *is* what we like to do; pleasure is what we *ought* to do." The next step is also guilty: The greatest degree of happiness *is* in "the greatest pleasure of the greatest number"; therefore we *ought* to seek "the greatest pleasure of the greatest number." Yet both Mill and Bentham considered that they had answered Hume's purely philosophical argument by introducing the reality of psychology. This *is* how we behave, and this is how we *ought* to behave. Psychological fact not only became moral duty, but the two were indivisible.

The Utilitarian argument appears all but self-evident to our twenty-first-century sensibilities. The fact is, we live in a Utilitarian age. The argument put forward by Bentham, and elaborated

by Mill, gradually found more and more con-
verts, until eventually it found the greatest pleasure with the greatest number. Twentieth-century
attempts to rebut it would prove disastrous.
Even on the rare occasions when this was tried,
the perpetrators had to pretend they were oper-
ating in its name. Communism in theory ap-
proved of it. As all the larger-than-life posters of
happy workers proclaimed, the greatest happiness for all lay in the future. Fascism in theory
appealed to a narrow racial version of it: the
happiness of being the all-conquering master
race. Both these proclaimed versions prove to be
travesties of Mill's liberal version.

The liberal Utilitarian idea, as developed by
Mill, spread through any society the more eman-
cipated it became. So much so that the principle
of utility now has the force of a basic constitutional right in all free, Western-style democracies. No politician would dream of contravening
it. Even exhortations to tighten our belts are always couched in terms of the common good,
which is understood as the pleasure to come.

Yet what precisely is this pleasure? What is it

that makes us happy? From the beginning, Mill was aware of the problem here. He recognized that the "utility," or pleasure, in Bentham's principle was far too narrow. Bentham had defined utility as "that property in any object whereby it tends to produce benefit, advantage, pleasure, good, or happiness . . . or . . . to prevent the happening of mischief, pain, evil, or unhappiness." This may have appeared broad enough, but the moment his felicific calculus was applied it became surprisingly simple and basic. Calculation was well equipped to take account of quantity, but where quality was concerned it was left wanting. And this was what happened in practice. For the most part, Bentham's utility was hedonistic only in terms of the lowest common denominator.

Mill's definition, on the other hand, takes in the notion of quality and progress: "it must be utility in the largest sense, grounded in the permanent interest of man as a progressive being." Implicit in this notion of happiness is the idea of things improving. Here Mill was in line with the very latest thinking of his age. Just two years before the publication of *Utilitarianism*, Darwin had published his *Origin of Species*. Mill's ideas of progress take account of evolution, but they nonetheless—strictly speaking—fall afoul of Hume's is/ought objection. (Progress *is* good for society / We *ought* to strive for progress.) In practice, this didn't seem to matter. Like pleasure, the idea of human progress would also be swallowed wholesale. This too our Utilitarian age has come to understand as a constitutional imperative. (Even so-called conservative parties feel the need to contradict their definition in the name of progress.)

Mill emphasizes that not all pleasures are of equal value. True happiness involves the higher pleasures of "spiritual perfection." In practice we are likely to prove more successful when we aim indirectly at achieving happiness. He stresses the effect of truth and beauty. These involve the cultivation of sensibility. Education, as well as experience, can bring about a deeper appreciation of happiness. In this way Mill's Utilitarianism rises above calculations of lowest-common-denominator hedonism. But it does have more than a whiff of elitism. Even the calculating Bentham had conceded that a man could sometimes be just as happy playing a simple game as listening to a profound symphony. "Prejudice apart, the game of push-pin is of equal value with the arts and sciences of music and poetry." Here his felicific calculus would seem to be relevant in *psychological* terms.

Yet Mill too was aware of this problem. He even made use of it to introduce a liberal note into Utilitarianism. The value of pleasure lies in the well-being it brings to individual lives. Yet alongside the interests of all must be aligned the consideration of all. There should be no coercion. Happiness best permeates a society when everyone is left to pursue his own version of happiness. The sole condition here should be that such individual versions of happiness do not interfere with those of other individuals, or with the general good. This introduction of liberalism overcomes the most frequent argument against "the greatest happiness of the greatest number." Taken literally, and to its limit, this argument would have Utilitarianism bringing back public hanging. By any consideration, the sadistic pleasure of the many would certainly outweigh the individual misery of the victim. Not so with Mill's noninterference version of happiness.

Mill's liberal interpretation of happiness—each to his own—introduces a further difficulty in the calculation of happiness, and its overall quantification. Happiness must now be interpreted, leaving it open to all manner of estimation. On the other hand, it can be argued that under these circumstances the calculation of individual happiness is neither possible nor necessary. How are we to assess the greatest happiness of the greatest number? Evidently a common-sense empirical standard would have to be used: an overall consensus.

This ties in with Mill's logic, making a unity of his empiricism, his liberalism, and his Utilitarianism. With everyone pursuing his own idea of happiness, the exploration of happiness would necessarily be empirical. So too would any estimation of the overall happiness. There would be no pre-fixed or transcendental notion. And any empirical calculation of the overall happiness would bear a remarkable similarity to enumerative induction. It would be open to error, but reiteration would reinforce its certainty. As Mill himself stated: "The sole evidence it is possible to produce that anything is desirable, is that people actually desire it." This may sound circular, but once again its psychology would seem to short-circuit Hume's is/ought objection. As Mill goes on to point out: "If the end which the utilitarian doctrine proposes to itself were not, in theory and in practice, acknowledged to be an end, nothing could ever convince any person that it was so."

But is this the entire picture? Surely we can occasionally choose to act in pursuit of something other than pleasure. We can act altruistically, or through a sense of duty. Mill concedes that we can will against our immediate inclination. But "doing the right thing" can also give us pleasure—in the form of pride in ourselves, joy at feeling a sense of our worth in the community, and so forth. In this way the cultivation of virtue can bring happiness to the individual and society. We thus arrive at a more profound conception of happiness, inclining us more toward "spiritual perfection."

Mill's emphasis on the individual pursuit of happiness allows the individual to develop himself in a fruitful and holistic manner. In this way he can become whole, exploring all his possibilities. Yet this is somewhat optimistic. Mill's formulation certainly *allows* for this to happen, but whether it will do so is another matter. Given free reign, our psychology does not always lead us into sweetness and light. It would take another generation before Freud explained the major part played in our individual lives by neurosis, the unconscious, and auto-destructive impulses. On the other hand, Mill's liberalism prevented paternalistic intervention in the behavior of others, with its assumption that most of us do not know what is for our own good. In Mill's time, even the most enlightened attempts at social amelioration were usually guided by this paternalistic principle: the wise and enlightened human being knows best. Bentham and Mill's father had certainly thought so. They might have proclaimed a belief in liberty, but this was to prove a highly ideal and theoretical concept, with little relevance to practice. Once again firsthand experience had led Mill to his conclusion. The individual had a right to his own freedom, and his own interpretation of this freedom.

It thus comes as no surprise that during this period Mill published his most influential work of political philosophy, *On Liberty*. In his introduction Mill explains that he is concerned not with the philosophical problem of free will and determinism but with "the nature and limits of the power which can be legitimately exercised by society over the individual." He goes on to state: "The struggle between Liberty and Authority is the most conspicuous feature in the portions of history with which we are earliest familiar," and he makes it clear that it remains a "conspicuous feature" of his contemporary society—though this was more the case in Europe than in England, where "owing to the peculiar circumstances of our political history . . . there is considerable jealousy of direct interference, by the legislative or the executive power, with private conduct." This was "not so much for any regard for the independence of the individual, as for the still subsisting habit of looking on the government as representing an opposite interest to the public." For this reason: "The majority have not learnt to feel the power of the government their power, or its opinions their opinions."

Mill asserts that there is just one "very simple principle" which should "govern absolutely the dealings of society with the individual in the way of compulsion and control." This is that "the sole end for which mankind are warranted, individually or collectively, in interfering with the liberty of action of any of their number, is self-protection." The "claim we have on our fellow-creatures to join in making safe for us the very ground work of our existence" is the only claim of justice—though he adds that society is obliged to provide "the essentials of well-being" for its citizens. Mill looked forward to an ideal Utilitarian state. Far from being an idealized utopia, this bears more than a partial resemblance to present-day society in much of the free world (though without a full prescience of the problems which can beset such a society).

Mill's Utilitarian state would ensure the social and economic conditions under which each individual could live according to his own ideas. The individual would thus be able to develop his full potential as a human being. Once again the emphasis is on progressive self-development, cultivating values and pursuing ends that enable the individual to fulfill his or her character. (As we shall see, Mill was no sexist: the Utilitarian society thrived on the happiness of *all* its citizens.)

Liberty is thus based on Utilitarian ideals. The citizen and the state do not come together in a "social contract," by means of which the citizen surrenders certain private rights in order to gain public rights. The social contract requires a surrender of liberty, whereas the Utilitarian ideal involves its private cultivation. Liberty and Utilitarianism had been linked from the start. Bentham's concept of liberty had not been entirely theoretical. His belief in the freedom of the individual had even led him to suggest that the law forbidding homosexuality should be repealed "How a voluntary act of this sort by two individuals can be said to have anything to do with the safety of them or any other individual whatever, is somewhat difficult to be conceived." Such advanced ideas were not widely promoted at a time when those "caught in buggery" ended up on the gallows. Bentham's opinion on homosexuality, especially coming from a man of high-minded principles who had no sexual experience whatsoever—he remained chaste throughout his life—speaks volumes for the liberalizing effect of his Utilitarianism. As Mill himself expressed it, in the chaste, generalized terms perhaps more befitting another lifelong virgin: "As it is useful that while mankind are imperfect there should be different opinions; so is it that there should be different experiments of living." (Indeed, in our modern Utilitarian society it is chastity itself that has come to be regarded as the outlandish "experiment of living.") But the last word on such contradictions should be Mill's: "Complete liberty of contradicting and disproving our opinions is the very condition which justifies us in assuming its truth for purposes of action; and on no other terms can a being with human faculties have any rational assurance of being right."

It is instructive to recall that the injustices of the society which inspired Mill to write these words were at the same time inspiring Marx to write *Das Kapital*. Many would see Marx's revolutionary anger as more pertinent to the grinding poverty and slums of Victorian Britain than Mill's lofty sentiments. Yet ironically it is Mill's ideas that continue to resonate with us. Seemingly ineffectual at the time, they would guide Western society to its present condition. And they are beginning to inform those states that have only recently emerged from the Marxist nightmare.

But were Mill's words really so ineffectual? In theory, at least, Mill's prescription was just as likely to cure the social ills of his time as Marx's. Mill advocated freedom to pursue individual goals: this was intended to liberate the individual's full potential, enabling us all to discover our own talents. Such freedom would give birth to creativity and imaginative development of our full potential. As a result we would be able to advance morally, spiritually, and intellectually. In its own way this would bring about a better society in which the ills that so angered Marx would be overcome—but without the drastic disruptions of revolution. Once again, Mill's proposals hardly appear to be a practical, effective way of solving the social and economic problems that plagued Victorian Britain. Even so, they may have determined precisely how much Western society did advance during the 150 years since Mill. The liberating effect of such ideas was at first very slow, but over the last half-century or so it has achieved considerable speed and success. The Silicon Valleys that are now found throughout the Western world are perfect examples of Mill's self-realization. And because they depend upon personal qualities and enterprise, they will certainly overcome temporary setbacks.

There remains one persistent criticism of Mill's liberal Utilitarianism. How do we calculate the general good: the greatest happiness of the greatest number? The provisional answer is empirical. Common sense and experience will show us the way. But even this leads to difficulties. The individual pursuit of happiness inevitably results in different versions of happiness, as Mill was all too aware. But this means that logically it is not possible to calculate any large-scale happiness in society. How can any prescription for a generalized happiness claim to bring happiness for all, when each has his own version of happiness? Do our individual versions of happiness in fact relate in any way to a society-wide definition of happiness? In terms of philosophical argument, the answer here is probably no. There is no logical reason why individual conceptions of happiness should have anything in common. But Utilitarians would argue that this is as irrelevant to the point as Hume's philosophical arguments. As human beings we do have the element of human nature in common, and this is wide enough to assume a loose consensus.

This is the "you know it makes sense" argument. And in practice this is how modern democratic liberalism—Utilitarian to the core—actually works. Economists calculate a generalized "feel-good" factor, usually based on the rate and amount of consumer spending. But in the end this is merely economics calculating on its own terms, for its own ends and for its own good. It may give us an *indication* of overall human happiness within a society, but it does not calculate actual happiness. This is a separate entity and is certainly not identical to the amount of money we spend: there is no necessary link between the two. Yet it seems that for the time being this is the best we can do. As our society is now predominantly governed by economic factors, it should come as no surprise that these factors are claimed to indicate how we are. We are in fact back to something very similar to Bentham's felicific calculus and its lowest-common-denominator syndrome.

The success of Mill's published works brought him to increasing public attention. He became a well-respected figure and used his renown to good effect on a number of issues of the day. When the American Civil War broke out in 1861, he was voiciferous in his support of the North. In his view the central issue was slavery, which had no place in any Utilitarian scheme of things. (As a young man Mill had strongly favored William Wilberforce's antislavery bill, which had passed the British Parliament almost thirty years earlier.)

In 1865 Mill himself was persuaded to stand for Parliament. But he told his Liberal party backers that he would do so only on his own somewhat unusual terms. During the election he would conduct no campaign and would allow no one to be paid to canvas on his behalf. Initially he even declined to give speeches or address the electorate in any way. In accordance with his liberal Utilitarian principles, he wished to allow the voters to make up their own minds on this matter. He was finally dissuaded from this rare political reticence and gave just one speech. After he had spoken, he answered the questions posed by his audience. Inevitably some of these questions were loaded—yet he answered with a beguiling honesty. At one point he was asked, "Did you declare that the English working classes, though differing from some other countries in being ashamed of lying, were yet 'generally liars'?" Mill immediately replied, "I did." The working-class members of the audience responded with appreciative applause, and Mill was duly elected.

During his time as a member of Parliament, Mill spoke out on a number of issues, including women's suffrage and government corruption. He gave expert advice on economic matters and added his weight to the passing of the 1867 Reform Bill. (This second major reform bill to pass through the British Parliament extended the franchise and doubled the size of the electorate.)

Despite such sterling work, in the election the following year Mill lost his seat to the successful news agent W. H. Smith. The sixty-two-year-old Mill retired to France, near Avignon, so that he could live close to the grave of his beloved Harriet. Here he was looked after by her daughter Helen, who became his constant companion (again, with no hint of any "impropriety"). But Mill's regard for his dead wife was more than the customary Victorian sentimentality. In pursuance of the cause they had both championed, Mill wrote *The Subjection of Women.* One of the earlier tracts on this issue, it carries through to their logical conclusion many of the points Mill had raised in *On Liberty*. Besides being all of a piece with his philosophy, this work also contains psychological insight. "So long as an opinion is strongly rooted in the feelings, it gains rather than loses in stability by having a preponderant weight of argument against it. For if it were accepted as a result of argument, the refutation of the argument might shake the solidity of the conviction; but when it rests solely on feeling, the worse it fares in argumentative contest, the more persuaded its adherents are that their feeling must have some deeper ground, which the arguments do not reach." Such insight applies well beyond the time and place of Mill's particular argument.

The Utilitarian argument for equality is evident and is backed by Mill's empiricism as well as his liberalism. But not all his arguments from his own experience carry quite such force for the modern woman. As a result of his rare relationship with Harriet, Mill felt bound to concede that women had no wish for the "animal function" of sex: men should refrain from attempting to inflict this noisome habit on "the weaker sex."

Mill spent the last few years of his life writing his *Autobiography*, whose openness and self-revelation are particularly evident in his feelings for his father. This remains one of the finest descriptions of what it is like to grow up as a "forced genius" and the effects of this on the sensibility concerned. His description of his "constitutionally irritable" father creates a true Victorian ogre. In an earlier draft of this work Mill tells how his father and mother "lived as far apart, under the same roof, as the north pole from the south." Much has been made of the fact that his mother Harriet had the same name as the love of his life, and this has led psychologists to a wide variety of more or less spurious conclusions. What is clear is that even as a child Mill knew, "Mine was not an education of love, but of fear." That he survived this, and survived it to become such a liberal and humanitarian figure, with so few hang-ups, is little short of a miracle. And even some who do not share Mill's sexual hang-ups may sympathize with his opinion: "Any great improvement in human life is not to be looked for as long as the animal instinct of sex occupies the absurdly disporportionate place it does." Alas, Freud was on the horizon—and human life would improve itself regardless.

Mill died at Avignon in 1873 at the age of sixty-six. His liberalism had not made him a popular figure among the Victorian bourgeoisie; similarly, his individualistic prescriptions had not chimed with the revolutionary notions of the left. Yet his death was mourned throughout Britain and beyond, wherever hypocrisy had not stifled compassion, wherever the belief in freedom extended beyond self-interest and self-opinion.

Afterword

Mill has suffered disproportionately at the hands of posterity. Philosophers tend to disparage his Utilitarianism as unoriginal, regarding him as a mere follower of Bentham. This is more than unfair. Mill's liberal development and widespread advocacy of Utilitarianism turned Bentham's philosophical ideas into a full-fledged coherent force, both in philosophy and in public life. Likewise Mill's liberal and political ideas have also suffered, largely because they have been so successful. What Mill advocated, in the face of strong public opinion to the contrary, now seems obvious to us. We live in a liberal, Utilitarian age. Acts of Congress, affective decisions of most kinds, even our private morality—all are subjected to Utilitarian testing. Consciously or unconsciously, we take many personal decisions and form our opinions with the Utilitarian slogan in mind. "The greatest benefit of the greatest number" is so potent as to be almost an unspoken founding principle of our modern way of life in the free Western democracies.

Yet it is precisely Mill's liberalism that remains contentious today. It is all very well being liberal in a liberal age, but what is to be done about society's ills? Mill was willing to grasp the nettle here. Even with regard to drunkenness, he stuck to his liberal, nonpaternalistic guns. Society did not have the right to press its members to adopt an "ordinary standard of rational behavior." He argued that during childhood and early adulthood society had "absolute power" over the individual. If it couldn't instill rational behavior during this period, it was society's own fault that its members behaved irrationally.

Two points strike against such liberalism today. First, our society is now plagued with drugs more than drunkenness. Addictive hard drugs would appear a far more potent and destructive "irrationality." On the other hand, Mill would probably argue—and with some justice—that drunkenness wreaked equal destruction in Victorian slums. Second, modern society certainly does not have "absolute power" over young adults. (And this is largely due to liberal attitudes toward education, upbringing, and the like.) Yet even if we find ourselves inclined to abandon certain aspects of Mill's liberalism, he still guides our thinking. Whatever we decided to put in place of such ineffectual liberalism will certainly be assessed according to Utilitarian principles. Mill may not always get our vote, but he still has the last word!

From Mill's Writings

The greatest happiness of the greatest number is the foundation of morals and legislation.

— Jeremy Bentham

Nature has placed mankind under the governance of two soveriegn masters, *pain* and *pleasure*. It is for them alone to point out what we ought to do, as well as to determine what we shall do. On the one hand the standard of right and wrong, on the other the chain of causes and effects, are fastened to their throne. They govern us in all we do, in all we say, in all we think; every effort we make to throw off our subjection will serve but to demonstrate and confirm it. In words a man may pretend to abjure their empire, but in reality he will remain subject to it all the while. . . . Systems which attempt to question it deal in sounds instead of sense, in caprice instead of reason, in darkness instead of light.

—Jeremy Bentham

Desiring a thing and finding it pleasant, aversion to it and thinking of it as painful, are phenomena entirely inseperable, or rather two parts of the same phenomena . . . to desire anything, except in proportion as the idea of it is pleasant, is a physical and metaphysical impossibility.

—John Stuart Mill, *Utilitarianism*

The objectors may perhaps doubt whether human beings, if taught to consider happiness as the end of life, would be satisfied with such a moderate share of it. But great numbers of mankind have been satisfied with much less. The main constituents of a satisfied life appear to be two, either of which by itself is often found suffi-

cient for the purpose: tranquillity, and excitement.
—John Stuart Mill, *Utilitarianism*

It is better to be a human being dissatisfied than a pig satisfied; better to be Socrates dissatisfied than a fool satisfied. And if the fool, or the pig, is of a different opinion, it is because they only know their own side of the question.
—John Stuart Mill, *Utilitarianism*

The object of this essay is to assert one very simple principle as entitled to govern absolutely the dealings of society with the individual in the way of compulsion and control, whether the means be physical force in the form of legal penalties, or the moral coercion of public opinion. That principle is, that the sole end for which mankind are warranted, individually or collecively, in interfering with the liberty of action of any of their number, is self-protection. The only purpose for which power can be rightfully exercised over any member of a civilized community, against his will, is to prevent harm to others. His own good, either physical or moral, is not a sufficient warrant. He cannot rightfully be compelled to do or forbear because it will be better for him to do so, because it will make him happier, because, in the opinions of others, to do so would be wise, or even right.

—John Stuart Mill, *On Liberty*

Over himself, over his own body and mind, the individual is sovereign.

—John Stuart Mill, *On Liberty*

If all mankind minus one were of one opinion, and only one person were of the contrary opinion, mankind would be no more justified in silencing that one person, than he, if he had the power, would be justified in silencing mankind.

—John Stuart Mill, *On Liberty*

As often as a study is cultivated by narrow minds, they will draw from it narrow conclusions.

—John Stuart Mill, *Auguste Comte and Positivism*

The true virtue of human beings is fitness to live together as equals; claiming nothing for themselves but what they as freely concede to everyone else; regarding command of any kind as an exceptional necessity, and in all cases a temporary one.

—John Stuart Mill, *The Subjection of Women*

Ask yourself whether you are happy, and you cease to be so.

—John Stuart Mill, *Autobiography*

Chronology of Significant Philosophical Dates

6th C B.C.	The beginning of Western philosophy with Thales of Miletus.
End of 6th C B.C.	Death of Pythagoras.
399 B.C.	Socrates sentenced to death in Athens.
c 387 B.C.	Plato founds the Academy in Athens, the first university.
335 B.C.	Aristotle founds the Lyceum in Athens, a rival school to the Academy.

324 A.D.   Emperor Constantine moves capital
                  of Roman Empire to Byzantium.

400 A.D.   St. Augustine writes his
                  Confessions. Philosophy absorbed
                  into Christian theology.

410 A.D.   Sack of Rome by Visigoths heralds
                  opening of Dark Ages.

529 A.D.   Closure of Academy in Athens by
                  Emperor Justinian marks end of
                  Hellenic thought.

Mid-13th C   Thomas Aquinas writes his
                  commentaries on Aristotle. Era of
                  Scholasticism.

1453   Fall of Byzantium to Turks, end of
                  Byzantine Empire.

1492   Columbus reaches America.
                  Renaissance in Florence and revival
                  of interest in Greek learning.

1543   Copernicus publishes *On the
                  Revolution of the Celestial Orbs*,
                  proving mathematically that the
                  earth revolves around the sun.

1633	Galileo forced by church to recant heliocentric theory of the universe.
1641	Descartes publishes his *Meditations*, the start of modern philosophy.
1677	Death of Spinoza allows publication of his *Ethics*.
1687	Newton publishes *Principia*, introducing concept of gravity.
1689	Locke publishes *Essay Concerning Human Understanding*. Start of empiricism.
1710	Berkeley publishes *Principles of Human Knowledge*, advancing empiricism to new extremes.
1716	Death of Leibniz.
1739–1740	Hume publishes *Treatise of Human Nature*, taking empiricism to its logical limits.
1781	Kant, awakened from his "dogmatic slumbers" by Hume, publishes *Critique of Pure Reason*.

	Great era of German metaphysics begins.
1807	Hegel publishes *The Phenomenology of Mind*, high point of German metaphysics.
1818	Schopenhauer publishes *The World as Will and Representation*, introducing Indian philosophy into German metaphysics.
1889	Nietzsche, having declared "God is dead," succumbs to madness in Turin.
1921	Wittgenstein publishes *Tractatus Logico-Philosophicus*, claiming the "final solution" to the problems of philosophy.
1920s	Vienna Circle propounds Logical Positivism.
1927	Heidegger publishes *Being and Time*, heralding split between analytical and Continental philosophy.
1943	Sartre publishes *Being and Nothingness*, advancing

Heidegger's thought and instigating existentialism.

1953   Posthumous publication of Wittgenstein's *Philosophical Investigations*. High era of linguistic analysis.

Chronology of Mill's Life and Times

1806   John Stuart Mill born in London on May 20.

1807   Wordsworth publishes *Poems in Two Volumes*. Hegel publishes his *Phenomenology of Spirit*.

1817   The precocious Mill begins writing a history of Rome under the instruction of his father, James Mill.

1824   Takes up post in East India Company.

1826   Suffers nervous breakdown.

1830	Falls in love with the married Harriet Taylor and continues platonic relationship owing to complaisance of her husband, John Taylor.
1832	First Reform Act.
1843	Publishes *System of Logic*.
1848	Revolutions break out throughout Europe. Marx and Engels publish *Communist Manifesto*. Mill publishes *System of Political Economy*.
1849	Harriet's husband, John Taylor, dies.
1851	Mill marries Harriet Taylor.
1857	The Indian Mutiny.
1858	East India Company dissolved. Mill retires on pension and travels to France with Harriet. Harriet dies of tuberculosis at Avignon in south of France.
1859	Darwin publishes *Origin of*

	Species. Mill publishes *On Liberty*.
1851	Outbreak of American Civil War: Mill encourages support for the North in the teeth of British public opinion. Publishes *Utilitarianism*.
1865	Elected Member of Parliament for Westminster.
1867	Second Reform Act passed by Parliament.
1868	Mill defeated in general election and loses seat in Parliament. Returns to Avignon, where he is looked after by his stepdaughter, Helen Taylor.
1869	Publishes *The Subjection of Women*. Opening of the Suez Canal.
1873	Mill dies at Avignon, aged sixty-six.

Recommended Reading

Maurice Cowling, *Mill and Liberalism* (Cambridge University Press, 1990). An in-depth study of this key subject which lies at the heart of all Mill's philosophical and political thinking.

John Stuart Mill, *Autobiography*, John Robson, ed. (Penguin, 1990). This highly revealing and intriguing work is best on the early years of his life, his education, and his difficult relationship with his father. Freudians will have a field day with this pre-Freudian work.

John Stuart Mill, *On Liberty, and Other Essays*, John Gray, ed. (Oxford University Press, 1998). Mill's short work outlining his liberal philosophical views in a political context. Parts of this book remain as relevant today as they were when it was first written.

John Stuart Mill, *Utilitarianism*, Roger Crisp, ed. (Oxford University Press, 1998). This shorter work offers Mill's own explanation and traces the development of the philosophy that he did so much to champion.

Michael St. John Packe, *The Life of John Stuart Mill* (Macmillan, 1954). Although long out of print, this biography contains the best account of Mill's life and is worth searching for. It provides sufficient personal and intellectual detail for you to make up your own mind.

John Skorupski, ed., *The Cambridge Companion to Mill* (Cambridge University Press, 1997). A wide range of essays covering almost all the topics dealt with by Mill in his long and industrious career. Ideal for following up in detail the philosophical aspects of his utilitarianism.

Index

A NOTE ON THE AUTHOR

Paul Strathern has lectured in philosophy and mathematics and now lives and writes in London. A Somerset Maugham prize winner, he is also the author of books on history and travel as well as five novels. His articles have appeared in a great many publications, including the *Observer* (London) and the *Irish Times*. His own degree in philosophy was earned at Trinity College, Dublin.

NOW PUBLISHED IN THIS SERIES:

Thomas Aquinas in 90 Minutes
Aristotle in 90 Minutes
St. Augustine in 90 Minutes
Berkeley in 90 Minutes
Confucius in 90 Minutes
Derrida in 90 Minutes
Descartes in 90 Minutes
Dewey in 90 Minutes
Foucault in 90 Minutes
Hegel in 90 Minutes
Heidegger in 90 Minutes
Hume in 90 Minutes
Kant in 90 Minutes
Kierkegaard in 90 Minutes
Leibniz in 90 Minutes
Locke in 90 Minutes
Machiavelli in 90 Minutes
Marx in 90 Minutes
J. S. Mill in 90 Minutes
Nietzsche in 90 Minutes
Plato in 90 Minutes
Rousseau in 90 Minutes
Bertrand Russell in 90 Minutes
Sartre in 90 Minutes
Schopenhauer in 90 Minutes
Socrates in 90 Minutes
Spinoza in 90 Minutes
Wittgenstein in 90 Minutes